OUR CRAFT BOOK

Foo Yihn & Foo Kwee Horng

Marshall Cavendish Editions

Published by Marshall Cavendish Editions
An imprint of Marshall Cavendish International

A member of the
Times Publishing Group

Other Marshall Cavendish Offices:
Marshall Cavendish Corporation, 800 Westchester Ave, Suite N-641, Rye Brook, NY 10573, USA • Marshall Cavendish International (Thailand) Co Ltd, 253 Asoke, 16th Floor, Sukhumvit 21 Road, Klongtoey Nua, Wattana, Bangkok 10110, Thailand • Marshall Cavendish (Malaysia) Sdn Bhd, Times Subang, Lot 46, Subang Hi-Tech Industrial Park, Batu Tiga, 40000 Shah Alam, Selangor Darul Ehsan, Malaysia

National Library Board, Singapore Cataloguing in Publication Data
Name(s): Foo, Yihn. | Foo, Kwee Horng, author.
Title: Our craft book / Foo Yihn & Foo Kwee Horng.
Description: Singapore : Marshall Cavendish Editions, [2023]
Identifier(s): ISBN 978-981-5066-76-0
Subject(s): LCSH: Handicraft--Juvenile literature.
Classification: DDC 745.5--dc23

Printed in Singapore

To my mother for believing in me, supporting my dreams, and listening to my stories.

—Yihn

To all parents who are making an effort to spend quality time with their children, may they be children or adults!

—Kwee Horng

Contents

The Sky 8

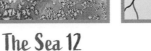

The Sea 12

Park 16

Garden 20

Aquarium 24

Florist 28

Airport 32

Marina 36

Train Station 40

Wonderland 44

Zoo 48

Estate 52

Introduction

This is a fun-filled activity book that introduces pre-school children to various places of interest. The activities can be done before a visit to familiarise the child to the place or as a post-visit activity to allow the child to express his response to the place.

Like in all art making activities, while there is a recommended product in the form of a painting or a 3D object, the main focus is on the creative process through the exploration of materials and the child's unique interpretation. The activities are designed to foster interaction between children and also with adults. While none of the activities are digital art based, referencing images of the place or taking pictures during the visits is highly recommended as they can be used to complement the art making.

The recommended age group is from 3-6 years old but no child or adult is too old to dabble in these activities as a form of creative artistic expression! As our target audience are young children, the instructions are kept short and simple. A polished and sophisticated outcome of the product (and that should not be measured by an adult's standards) is not our emphasis too but something which a child would find doable.

There is no specific mention of things like types of brushes or palettes for paints because such things are probably laying around the house and with some ingenuity, no equipment and materials will be too difficult to source. The basic skills involved such as cutting, pasting, drawing and painting are required but the child who is not extremely skilled will also be able to embark on the activities with some help from an adult and with lots of encouragement, the latter being the most important!

The activities are meant to inspire and they can certainly lead to new discoveries and interpretations, such as a pom pom octopus or a futuristic metropolis! We had fun coming up with the activities and working on them despite being two adults way over the recommended age for this book so we hope that the book will do the same for your child and you, hence the title *Our Craft Book*.

Skills highlighted: Painting and Collage

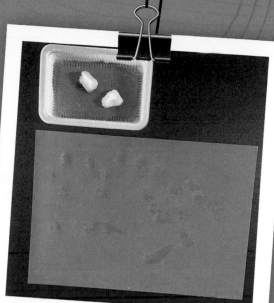

Step 1

Dip cotton balls in paint and stamp them on the paper

Materials

- Blue construction paper
- Grey paint
- White glue
- Cotton balls
- Tissue paper (optional)

*Outcome

Tip 1: Try spacing out the prints
Tip 2: Cover about half the paper

Step 2
Paste cotton balls on the paper using glue

Done!

Variation: Tissue paper clouds

Look at the sky, what shapes do you see?

Shape the tissue paper to form clouds and paste them on the paper

Skills highlighted: Drawing and Painting

Materials

- Drawing paper
- Blue watercolour paint
- Candles
- Paint brush
- Salt

Step 1

Draw wavy lines on the paper using candles

Tip: Press harder for more visible lines

Alternatively, use while oil pastels

Step 2

Paint over the paper with paint

Step 3
Sprinkle salt over paper while paint is still wet

Step 4
Wait for paper to dry and watch the magic happen!

14

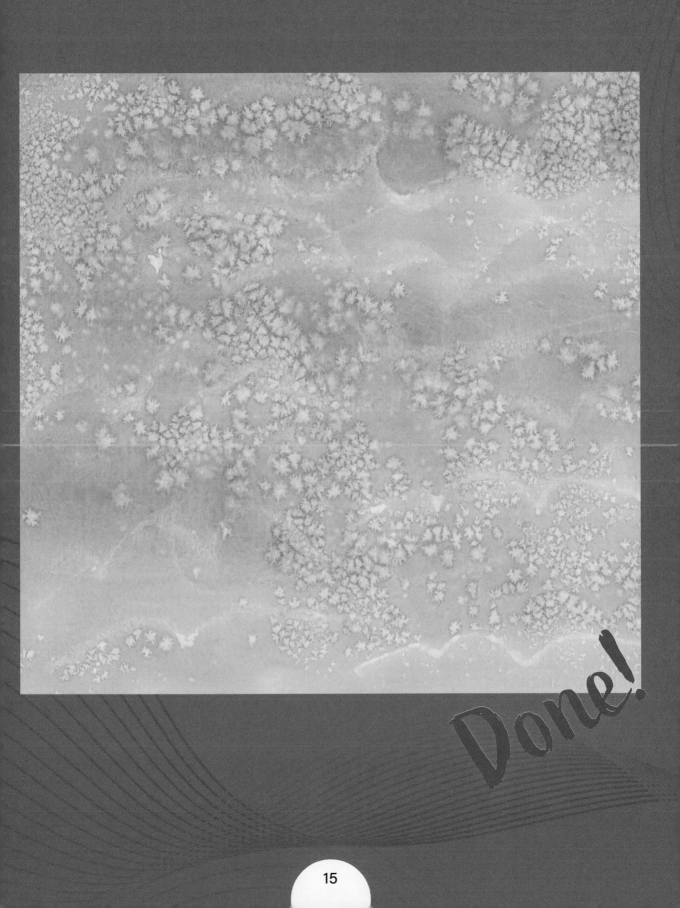

Done!

Skills highlighted: Drawing, Painting and Printing

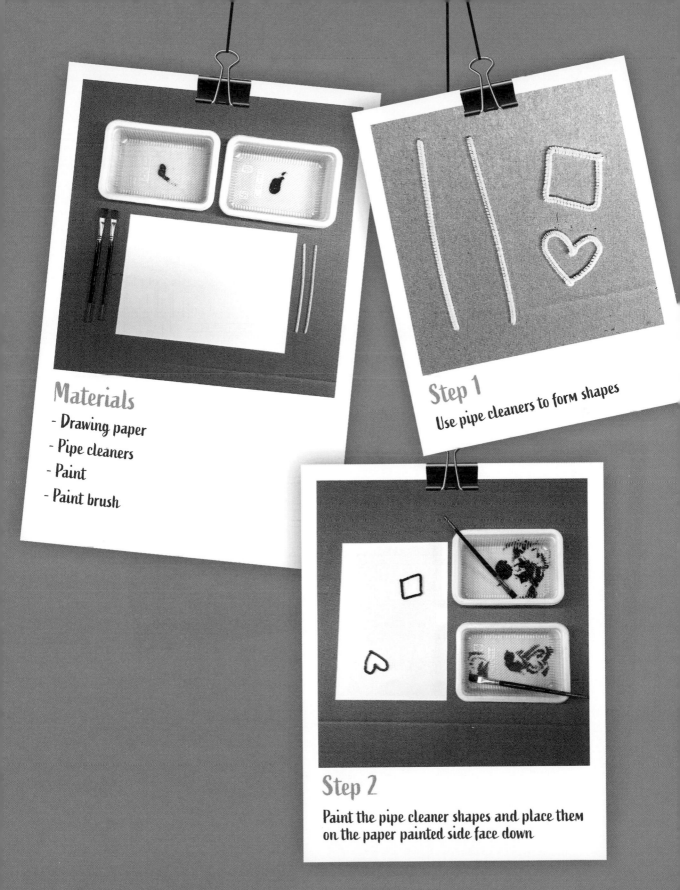

Materials

- Drawing paper
- Pipe cleaners
- Paint
- Paint brush

Step 1

Use pipe cleaners to form shapes

Step 2

Paint the pipe cleaner shapes and place them on the paper painted side face down

Step 3

Place another piece of paper on top of the first for easy printing

Press gently over the pipe cleaner shapes

Step 4

Add patterns using markers or colour pencils

Tip: Do not forget the kite string

Done!

Optional: Cut out kites and add to "The Sky"

Skills highlighted: Painting and Printing

Materials

- Drawing paper
- Dark watercolour paint
- Straw
- Paint brush
- Coloured paints

Step 1

Drop a few drops of paint on the paper

Step 2

Blow the paint drops with a straw

Tip: Use a shorter and narrower straw for younger children

Step 3

Print 'flowers' using your finger tips

Tip: Wait for 'branches' to dry before printing flowers

Skills highlighted: Drawing and Painting

Materials

- Drawing paper
- Oil pastels
- Shoe or slipper

Optional

- Scissors
- White glue

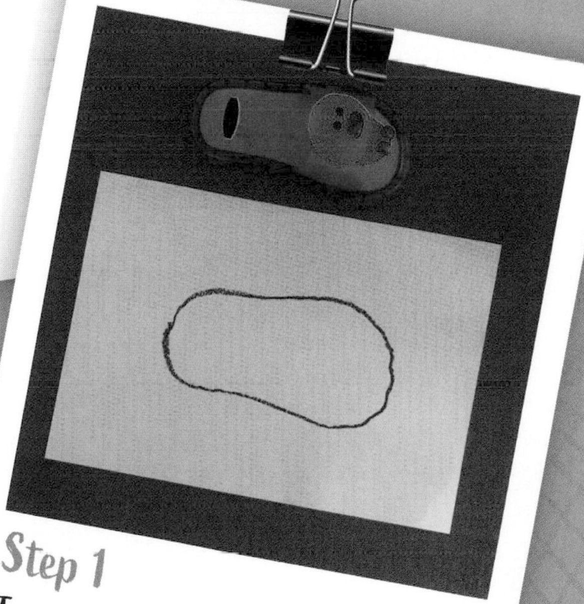

Step 1

Trace shoe or slipper outline on the paper with oil pastels

Body parts of a fish

The five types of fins (see if you can remember them), eyes and mouth

Labels on fish diagram: dorsal fin, eye, mouth, pectoral fin, pelvic fin, anal fin, caudal fin

Step 2

Draw in the parts of the fish and add colour
Tip: prompt for the number of fins

Done!

Optional: Cut out the fish and add to "The Sea"
Add paper "seaweed"

Skill highlighted: 3D

Materials

- Yarn
- Hard card
- Straw
- Tape
- Scissors

Step 1

Tape a length of yarn on a hard card

Tip: The width of the card should be equal to the size of the pom pom

Tip 2: Make the length of yarn longer than the straw

Step 2

Coil yarn around the hard card

Tip: More coils make a fatter pom pom

Suggestion: 50 coils

Step 3

Tie a double knot

Step 4

Remove coils from the hard card and tie
another double knot for the other side

Step 5

Cut the coils around the edge

Tip: Trim yarn if needed to make the
pom pom rounder

Step 6

Thread length of yarn through the straw

Pull yarn tight and tape end to straw

Done!

Skills highlighted: 3D and Painting

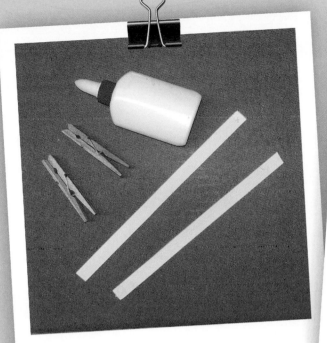

Materials

- Clothes pegs
- Paint
- Glue
- Hard card

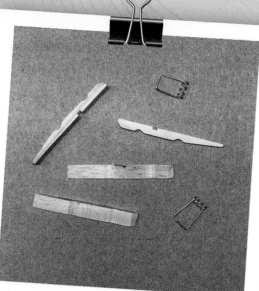

Step 1

Remove the springs
Tip: Adults can help with this

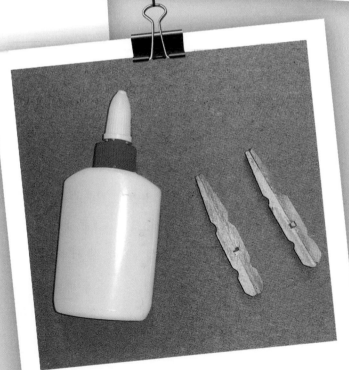

Step 2

Glue flat sides together

Step 3 Paint clothes pegs in any colour

Step 4 Add wings, vertical and horizontal rear tails using hard card

34

Done!

Optional: Place planes on 'The Sky' or hang as mobiles

Skills highlighted: 3D

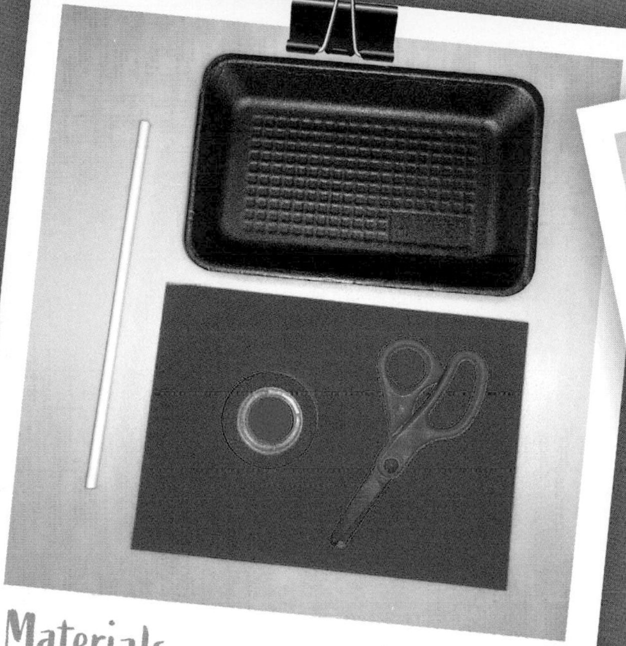

Materials

- Foam tray
- Tape
- Paper
- Straw
- Scissors

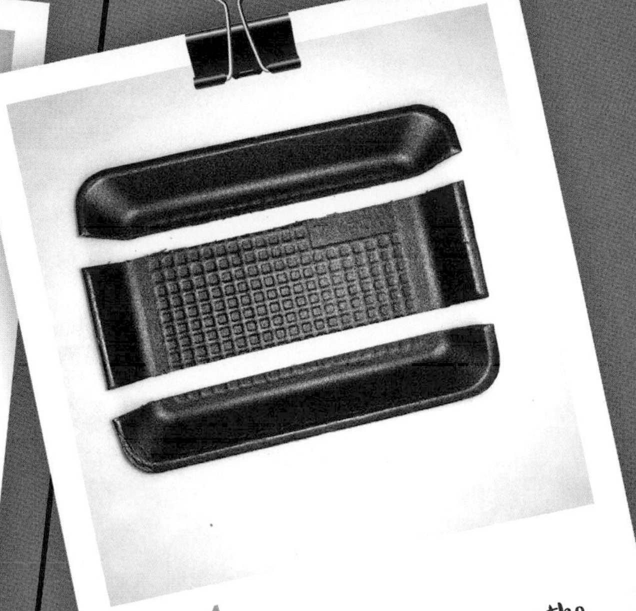

Step 1

Cut foam tray length-wise to reduce the width

Tips: Adults can help with this

Step 2

Tape the two parts together

Step 3

Wrap paper around the straw, tape and cut to the shape of sail

Make two cross cuts on the end of straw

Step 4

Fix straw with sail to the foam tray using tape or glue

Done!

Optional: Place boat on "The Sea"

Skills highlighted: Drawing and Painting

Materials

- Small paper boxes
- Glue
- Ice-cream sticks
- Hard card
- Paper
- Scissors

Step 1

Turn paper boxes inside out

Add "windows and doors" using coloured papers or stickers

Step 2

Paste ice-cream sticks and hard card to make rails

Tip: Test width of train carriage before pasting tracks or leave them unpasted

Done!

Optional: Add "grass" or sign posts to name the station

Skill highlighted: 3D

Materials

- Paper plate
- Kitchen roll core
- Pipe cleaners
- Paper strips
- Scissors
- Hole puncher

Step 1

Punch holes around the paper plate

Tip: A good opportunity to talk about the clock face

* 12 holes are recommended

Step 2

Secure pipe cleaners to plate using a simple bend to the pipe cleaner

Step 3

Decorate the kitchen roll core

Tip: You can also use two toilet roll cores to get the height

Step 4

Cut paper strips and punch a hole to make seats

Step 5

Arrach seats to the pipe cleaners

Tips: A simple bend to the pipe cleaner will do

Done!

Step 6

Assemble by glueing the core to the paper plates

Skill highlighted: 3D

Materials

- Pom poms big and small
- Pipe cleaners
- Plastic googly eyes
- Glue
- Scissors

Step 1

Glue eyes to small pom pom

Insert pipe cleaners for ears and nose

Optional: Use construction papers for eyes and ears instead

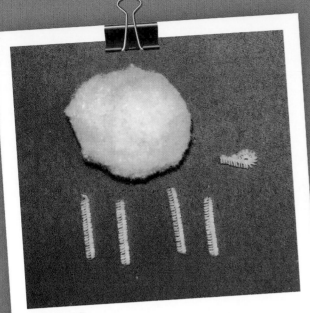

Step 2

Use four-lengths of pipe cleaners for the legs

Add another piece of pipe cleaner for the tail

Step 3

Glue "head" to "body"

Insert legs and tail

Tip: Glueing of pipe cleaners to pom pom is optional

Done!

How about adding a blue lamb?

or a blue baby elephant?

Skill highlighted: 3D

Materials

- Paper boxes of different sizes
- Coloured paper strips
- Coloured ink markers
- Glue
- Scissors

Step 1

Decorate buildings with paper strips and coloured ink markers

Tip: Adults can help by turning the boxes inside out first

Adding trees

- Clothes pegs
- Crepe paper

Step 2

Peg one end of crepe paper strip

Coil the strip and tuck the other end in or glue it

Tip: Use a darker and a lighter strip together

Lollipop trees?

Adding "The Sky", green pom pom shrubs and a toy car

Tips: Plan your estate, move the buildings around,
add more trees and shrubs

ABOUT THE AUTHORS

Foo Yihn is a pre-school teacher and a crafts entrepreneur. The design of this book was based primarily on her signature white frame and alphabet tiles (IG@Yihndulgence).

Foo Kwee Horng is a retired school art teacher and art supervisor for trainee art teachers. He now paints full-time but will occasionally work on meaningful projects such as this (IG@artfooart).